Disclaimer:

This work may not be copied, sold, used as content in any manner or your name put on it without consulting me. Every effort has been made to be accurate in this publication. The publisher does not assume any responsibility for errors, omissions or contrary interpretation. I do my best to provide the best information on the subject, but just reading it does not guarantee success. You will need to apply every step of the process in order to get the results you are looking for.

This publication is not intended for use as a source of any legal, medical or accounting advice. The information contained in this guide may be subject to laws of South Africa and other jurisdictions. I suggest carefully reading the necessary terms of the services/products used before applying it to any activity which is, or may be, regulated. I do not assume any responsibility for what you choose to do with this information. Use your own judgment.

Any perceived slight of specific people or organizations, and any resemblance to characters living, dead or otherwise, real or fictitious, is purely unintentional.

Some examples of past results are used in this publication; they are intended to be for example purposes only and do not guarantee you will get the same results. Your results may differ from mine. Your results from the use of this information will depend on you, your skills and effort, and other different unpredictable factors.

It is important for you to clearly understand that all marketing activities carry the possibility of loss of investment for testing purposes. Use this information wisely and at your own risk.

Table of Contents

Introduction	04
Section 1: Facebook Marketing Basics	
Chapter 1: What is Facebook all about	07
Chapter 2: What are Facebook Ads?	10
Chapter 3: What Is Retargeting And What Makes Facebook The Top Retargeting Platform?	13
Chapter 4: How can your business benefit from Facebook Ads	16
Section 2: Marketing on Facebook – Step by Step	
Chapter 5: Shocking Ad Facts To Consider	20
Chapter 6: Facebook Walkthrough	23
Chapter 7: Facebook Ads Manager Walkthrough	26
Chapter 8: Creating A Facebook Page To Run Ads	30
Chapter 9: Promoting A Basic Page Post The Right Way	34
Chapter 10: Creating a basic ad using the ads manager	39
Chapter 11: Creating A Custom Audience	45
Section 3: Advanced Facebook Marketing Strategies	
Chapter 12: Adding The Facebook Pixel From A Campaign To Your Business Website	49
Chapter 13: Sending More Traffic To Your Site With Facebook Ads	53
Chapter 14: Increasing Conversion Through The Ads Manager	58

Chapter 15: Creating A Facebook Retargeting Campaign	61
Chapter 16: Creating A Lead-Generation Funnel	64

Section 4: Additional Tips to consider

Chapter 17: Do's and Don'ts	68
Chapter 18: Premium tools and Services to consider	72
Chapter 19: Shocking Case Studies	76
Chapter 20: Frequently Asked Questions	80
Conclusion	**84**
Top Resources	**85**
Special Offer	**86**

Introduction:

Welcome to the latest and very easy to apply "Facebook Ads 3.0" Training, designed to take you by the hand and walk you through the process of getting the most out of Facebook Ads for your business.

I'm very excited to have you here, and I know that this will be very helpful for you.

This exclusive training will show you step-by-step, topic by topic, and tool by tool, what you need to know to dominate Facebook Ads, in the easiest way possible, using the most effective tools and in the shortest time ever.

This training is comprised of 20 chapters organized into 4 sections. This is exactly what you are going to learn:

Section 1: Facebook Ads Basics

In Chapters 1 through 5, we'll talk about:

- ✓ What Is Facebook All About?
- ✓ What Are Facebook Ads?
- ✓ What Is Retargeting And What Makes Facebook The Top Retargeting Platform?
- ✓ How Can Facebook Ads Help Your Business?
- ✓ Shocking Facebook Ad Facts To Consider

Section 2: Facebook Ads – Step by Step

In Chapters 6 through 10, we'll talk about:

- ✓ Facebook Walkthrough
- ✓ Facebook Ads Manager Walkthrough
- ✓ Creating A Facebook Page To Run Ads
- ✓ Promoting A Basic Page Post The Right Way
- ✓ Creating A Basic Ad Using The Ads Manager

Section 3: Advanced Facebook Ad Strategies

In Chapters 11 through 16, we'll talk about:

- ✓ Creating A Custom Audience
- ✓ Adding The Facebook Pixel From A Campaign To Your Business Website
- ✓ Sending More Traffic To Your Site With Facebook Ads
- ✓ Increasing Conversions Through The Ads Manager
- ✓ Creating A Lead-Generation Funnel
- ✓ Creating A Facebook Retargeting Campaign

Section 4: Additional Tips to consider

In Chapters 17 through 20, we'll talk about:

- ✓ Do's and Don'ts
- ✓ Premium tools and Services to consider
- ✓ Shocking Case Studies
- ✓ Frequently Asked Questions

Well, it's time for you to start getting the most out of Facebook Ads On behalf of your Business. I know you'll love this training.

Section 1

Chapter 1: What is Facebook all about

So let's get started by answering this question: What is Facebook actually all about? Well, Facebook is a social media network designed with straightforward social interaction in mind.

What has made Facebook such a popular platform is its ease of use and its wide variety of features and applications. Simply put, Facebook owes a lot of its popularity to its accessibility and how entertaining it is to use.

The main focus of the Facebook platform is in allowing its users to create online social profiles that they can populate with personal info, and that they can use to get in touch with others.

This is possible because Facebook users can connect with one another by adding friends to their social network.

The platform's popularity combined with its accessibility has made it the perfect platform to locate old friends at a distance and to meet new people. People can also use Facebook to play games, to chat with their Facebook friends and to share video content, all without leaving the site!

Facebook users can also create and share photo albums, comment on other people's profiles, and create Facebook "groups", which families and groups of friends use to share content privately.

Facebook is also an attractive platform for businesses because it offers companies, organizations and businesses across all industries to reach an audience of almost 2 billion active users a month.

The very social nature of the Facebook platform makes it the perfect channel for any business to reach and engage with a qualified pool of potential clients. Businesses can create their own Facebook profiles in the form of Facebook pages.

Facebook pages are designed to allow businesses, companies, brands, organizations, artists and the like to upload content to the platform the same way that any regular user would.

But there's more: Facebook Pages allow businesses to promote and market their products and services through Facebook's own advertising platform. Want to learn more? Tune in for the following chapter!

Chapter 2: What are Facebook Ads?

So far you knew Facebook as that social media website that everybody is using nowadays, up until i showed you that there's a lot more than meets the eye in my previous chapter, and it is about time to go a bit deeper.

As a regular user you might not be aware of a lot of the stuff that happens in the background because, for example, do you know how companies actually get discovered on the platform?

Yes, it is true that Facebook pages can do a lot of the work because you can find any type of content throughout Facebook by using the right keywords, but businesses won't be easily found organically if they're not already popular.

If you want to reach a broader audience for your business, you will need to do more than creating a Facebook page. Namely, you will need to advertise your business, and Facebook has that covered.

Facebook ads are advertising units that are shown to Facebook users on the Facebook advertising network. The Facebook advertising network is Facebook's response to the increasingly growing world of advertising platforms.

I am pretty sure that you have seen Facebook ads yourself, even without realizing it. Have you noticed that you have come across certain posts from pages that you do not follow on your Facebook timeline?

That right there is a Facebook ad targeted at you specifically, and when you "like" a sponsored post or start following the Facebook page promoting the post, then the advertising objective has been achieved by the advertiser.

And that is the power of Facebook ads. Facebook ads blend naturally across users' timelines on desktop and mobile devices without being intrusive, whereas advert units on other advertising networks such as the Google ad network can be easily spotted as ads, and are pretty much ignored because of that.

Facebook ads are great because they retain the very same elements that make any other Facebook post so engaging:

- ✓ Most Facebook Ads have a title just like any other regular page post

- ✓ Facebook ads have their own image, and they're cheaper than Display ads on most advertising networks

- ✓ Facebook ads include their own ad copy space, and because Facebook ads are mostly crafted as regular posts their copy helps them to blend incredibly well among all the content on a user's feed

- ✓ Lastly, Facebook ads have their own engagement cue, which depends on the objective set by the advertiser during set up. These engagement cues include like buttons, shop buttons, link buttons and more

What's more, Facebook ads are served on the basis of user activity and profile, which means that such ads are targeted to users according to demographic information, entertainment preferences, devices, and partner-supplied data through behavioral tracking.

That means that Facebook ads are based on what they do, on what they like, and on who they interact with on Facebook, making Facebook ads perhaps the most finely targeted option for advertisers.

But Facebook advertising goes beyond that, and it can help businesses to reach out to potential customers who are not engaged the first time. Want to learn more? Tune in to the following chapter!

Chapter 3: What Is Retargeting And What Makes Facebook The Top Retargeting Platform?

Let's take this training one step further right now. Let's talk about an advertising strategy so awesome and advanced that only a handful of marketers get it right.

You know how you have to pay top dollar to reach a certain percentage of your desired audience only to have them abandon your offers right after landing on your business site from your ads? And how bad does it feel to know that you might have lost a potential customer forever?

Well, what if i tell you that there is a way to track and reach those potentially lost customers once again, and what if i tell you that it really works? Wonder no more, because you are about to discover all about it!

What is Retargeting?

Retargeting, also referred to as "remarketing" in some instances, is an online advertising method that allows advertisers to stay relevant to bounced traffic. In other words, retargeting is an advertising strategy that will allow you to reach your leads long after they have clicked through your ads or visited your website.

How Does retargeting Work?

Retargeting works on the basic principle of following your potential audience across the internet. It "follows" your audience because, unlike traditional advertising, which advertisers use to show adverts to users on fixed channels, it tracks visitors and shows them adverts wherever they go.

OK, but how can you track and follow visitors with retargeting? Easy enough: You insert a code on your website which it's function is to save a cookie on your visitors' browsers.

This code is provided by the retargeting network, and the cookie that it inserts on the visitor's browsers will allow the retargeting provider to know when to serve ads to said visitors.

As you can see, what retargeting will allow you to do in turn is to serve ads to people that have already visited your website, which means that they're more likely to respond to those ads because they have already demonstrated interest.

Retargeting is used by many online marketers as a complimentary advertising strategy, because they can send people to the business website that they are promoting through a common advert unit and then to retarget those same users through retargeted adverts.

What Makes Facebook The Top Retargeting Platform?

There are a lot of different retargeting platforms out there, but Facebook is the only one that will allow you to retarget a unique custom audience, and to also reach its wide user base of more than 2 billion active people a month.

One of the most powerful retargeting features offered by Facebook is that it will also reach out to Facebook users that are similar to your retargeted audience.

Also, retargeted Facebook ads will be served to users right on their Facebook feeds on desktop and on mobile devices, making its retargeted ads less intrusive and easier for users to engage with. How far can you take your profits with all this? Let's find out in the next chapter!

Chapter 4: How can your business benefit from Facebook ads?

It is no longer a secret that Facebook is by far the social media platform of choice for online marketers for reasons that are not obvious up until you start using it to promote your business.

I already talked about Facebook's large and active worldwide audience, and that right there is an enormous benefit for any business because of exposure, and the good news is that businesses can create their own profiles as Facebook pages.

Then i talked about Facebook's advertising platform and how it works to help businesses to easily achieve their marketing objectives. Thanks to non-intrusive and retargeted ads, the Facebook Ads platform is one of the best options there is for advertisers.

Now i want to talk about how Facebook Ads can help your business to grow. These are some of the most under reported yet more relevant benefits offered by the Facebook advertising network for businesses.

Facebook Ads are cost-effective

One of the reasons why the majority of businesses have a difficult time breaking through online is because of costs, mainly the cost of paid advertising, which can easily eat most of a business' marketing budget on a whim.

The Facebook Ads platform is one of the cheapest advertising options not only among online advertising networks but also when compared to any other form of advertising period. You can easily assign $15 to your advertising budget on any given day and reach 1,000 people. It doesn't get cheaper than that anywhere else!

Your potential customers are already spending lots of time on Facebook

Close to 80% of internet users use Facebook, and a good chunk of them are using it daily, and i guarantee you that a good portion of your target audience is in that 80%, which means that they're pretty much likely to interact with your advertising at any given moment.

Facebook Ads are the most targeted form of online advertising

Facebook ads are perhaps the only ones that will allow you to target a very much exact match of your target audience because they will allow you to advertise to people according to their age, their locations, their interests and other behaviors.

Facebook Ads drive results FAST

Facebook ads will give you immediate results because of their wide reach. This means that after one or two days of running ads on Facebook you will be able to determine whether your campaigns are being successful or need optimizations.

Facebook Ads increase brand awareness

Facebook Ads are better at creating brand awareness than any other advertising network because they allow your business to connect with people on a more personal level through Facebook pages. Increased brand awareness means more engagement, which in turn increases sales and profits!

Facebook Ads increase website traffic

Facebook Ads will allow you to set up click-to-website campaigns to increase traffic to your website, which can improve brand recall for your business.

Facebook Ads increase repeat business

You can use Facebook Ads to advertise to existing customers by importing their emails and personal data such as names or locations to Facebook Ad campaigns so you can reach them directly on their Facebook feeds.

Tune in to our next chapter so i can show you some exciting facts about Facebook advertising that will entice you further to start using Facebook Ads today!

Section 2

Chapter 5: Shocking Ad Facts To Consider

Digital advertising is outranking traditional advertising, and Facebook is at the top, as it currently dominates three quarters of the total digital advertising market.

Mobile currently makes up for 66% of Facebook's advertising revenue, which means that more than half of people responding positively to Facebook Ads are using mobile devices.

There are more than 40 million active business accounts on Facebook, mainly because of how accessible a platform Facebook is for small businesses operating on a tight budget and its low entry for advertisers.

Ad clicks on Facebook are increasing by a whopping 70% year by year, and click-through rates are growing by a rate of 160%, which only means that Facebook ads are becoming an excellent option when it comes to engagement to ROI ratio.

Facebook ads are sensitive to seasons. Mainly, they are sensitive to commerce heavy seasons such as Christmas and black Friday, when click through rates and cost per impressions increase steadily because advertisers are forced to increase their bids in order to be able to reach their target audiences. This is due to the high amount of people shopping during those seasons, which means that advertisers are competing to reach their potential customers.

The Facebook algorithm for ads favorites ads where images feature little to no text. The less text an ad image has the greater its chances to be served. In fact, Facebook has an image-to-text ratio that it uses to classify ad images according to how much text they feature, and awarding images with little to no text with higher distribution and lower cost per impressions.

Facebook collects close to 10,000 data points from each user. These data points are collected from the mundane information given by the users themselves such as their locations, names, jobs, and interests, as well as from partnerships with agencies that collect data from credit card companies, for example. It also collects data points from tracking users through cookies, and these data points are used for, you guessed right, targeting users with advertising. This same data is what will allow you to reach the right type of lead for your business, so any business not actively advertising on Facebook is missing out on something big.

On that same note, Facebook ad campaigns that target their audience using the Custom Audience targeting format get 387% greater conversion rates than ad campaigns using demographic targeting only. That means that using Facebook Ad's powerful targeting options you will get conversion rates almost 400% higher than on any other advertising platform.

Users aged 25 to 34 comprise 29% of Facebook's user base, and it so happens that this age bracket is the one where people spend the most on online based offers and products, so make sure to target this age bracket on your custom audiences.

Facebook made $3.69 billion in 2015. Facebook makes money from advertising, which means that it earned almost $4 billion out of advertisers in that year alone, which in turn means that marketers DO LOVE Facebook, and that means that Facebook Ads work.

Tune in to the following section, where i am going to teach you all the basics about getting started with Facebook Ads!

Chapter 6: Facebook Walkthrough

I am pretty sure that you already have a Facebook account and that you know how to use it for basic social networking, but in order to teach you all about the Facebook Ads platform, i also need to give you a complete overview of what you will find inside a Facebook account.

And it all starts when you sign in to your Facebook account and land on the home page. This is perhaps the part of Facebook that you are the most familiar with, so let's start from here.

On the home page you will have access to several tabs and buttons that will lead you to every other feature offered by your Facebook account. The first thing to note is Facebook's feed, which is where all the most recent updates from friends and pages will be shown to you.

Here in the feed is where Facebook ads such as promoted posts will be served as well. Ok, so right on top of the timeline is the post box, which is where you will be able to create your own posts and updates.

Note that only page posts are eligible for promotion, but i will show you how to set them up later on, so for now let's continue with the walkthrough. From this post box you can also create a photo or video album, or to launch a live video session using the "live video" feature. Let's now move to the upper right panel.

You can access your profile by clicking on the profile tab with your name and your picture. On your profile you will be able to see your "timeline", to click on "about" to add and modify your personal info, to click on "friends" to manage your contacts, to click on "photos" to manage your pictures and your photo albums, and to click on "more" to discover detailed information about the things you have liked and followed on the platform.

You can also easily change your profile picture by clicking on the "update your profile picture" button under your current profile picture and to add a cover photo by clicking on the "add a cover photo" button.

Now, by clicking on the "home" tab you can go back to Facebook's home page. By clicking on the "find friends" tab you can see your friend requests, your friend recommendations, and to actually look for people on Facebook using detailed filtering options in the "search for friends" box.

The icons beside this panel represent your notifications: new "friend requests", new "messages", and new "notifications. The question mark icon is a "quick help" access and right beside it you will find the account options menu.

By clicking on it, you will be able to see your pages, to create pages, to manage pages, to create and find groups, to create ads and access the Facebook advertising platform, to view your activity log, to set up news feed preferences, to access your account settings and to log out of Facebook.

Now, on the lower right corner you will find the Facebook chat, which is the platform's powerful instant messaging tool. You can click on it to see your online contacts and click on them to start a chat, and you can easily turn your chat off when busy with your marketing tasks.

Let's now look at the left side menu on the home page. This menu features several shortcuts to basically every feature available on Facebook, including "groups", "events", "games", "live video", "pages feed", "saved", "buy and sell groups" and "explore feed", among others.

Lastly, you will be able to use the "search" bar on top to use Facebook as a search engine. You will have to enter a keyword in it and then to either click on the search button or to click on any of the suggestions based on the keyword that you entered.

Once in the search results page you will be able to refine your search by "posts", "people", "photos", "videos", "shop", "pages", "places", "groups", "apps", "events" and "links", and you can filter your results according to criteria unique to each type of results, such as filtering by "category" if you refine your search using "pages".

As you can see, Facebook is a pretty powerful platform that you can use for more than every day social networking. In the following chapter I will, be taking you on a real time tour of the Facebook Ads manager account inside your Facebook account, so tune in!

Chapter 7: Facebook Ads Manager Walkthrough

Let's continue right where we left on our last chapter, because this time around i am going to give you a walk through a different part of Facebook, and it all starts right from your Facebook account.

That is right, i am going to walk you through the Facebook Ads manager, from where you will be able to create and manage your Facebook ads. This is the first step in your Facebook ads journey.

So start by clicking on the menu button on top and then on the "create ads" option. Then you will have to wait for Facebook to prepare your ad account, to connect to your pages, and to finish getting everything ready for you.

Now you will land in the ads manager main dashboard, from where you are going to be able to access all the Facebook ad features offered by your account. As you can see, the ads manager is first and foremost optimized to create ads right from the get go.

The main dashboard is organized for you to create an ad right when you feel like it. The first step is outlined above in the "campaign" box, where you can either "create new campaign" or "use existing campaign" by clicking on either tab.

Right below the campaign selection box you have the "what's your marketing objective" section, where you will be able to select your advertising objective, and on the left hand menu you have an outline of each step in the ad creation process.

From top to bottom these are "campaign", "ad account", "ad set", and "ad". I am going to go through these in detail in a following chapter, so let's continue checking out the ads manager. Let's proceed by taking a look at the options in the top bar menu from right to left.

First you will have a "help" tab, which you can click to get a condensed help summary with tips about using your Facebook ads account. Right next to it is the "settings" tab, and clicking on it will lead you to the "settings" section.

In this section you will be able to configure your "ad account setup" from the "ad accounts" tab. This account setup includes your "ad account id", which can't be changed, your "ad account name", your "time zone" and "currency" configurations, and your "advertising purpose" which you can set as "yes, i am buying ads for business purposes" or as "no, i am not buying ads for business purposes",

Then you will have your "business country". Now, in the "ad agency" menu you will need to specify whether you are an agency buying ads on behalf of an advertiser or not. In this tab you will also be able to configure your account's "attribution" and to add "ad account roles" if more people besides you are managing this ad account.

In the "pages" tab you will be able to check and manage your Facebook pages, on the "payment settings" you will be able to see your current bills, to "add a payment method", and to "set up your account spending limit", which is a useful feature in case that you are on a tight budget, and you will need to set your limit amount in the "account spending limit" field and click on "set limit".

Finally, in the "notifications" tab you will be able to activate or deactivate "all ad account notifications", to specify which "ad email notifications" you want to receive and what type of ad notifications you would like to receive directly on Facebook.

OK, so going back to the top bar menu you will find two notification icons. The first one to the right is the "pages" notifications icon, and the one next to it is the general "notifications" icon. Now, the account icon with your profile picture will allow you to switch between ad accounts if you have added more than one, to log out of your ad account and to go back to your newsfeed.

You will be able to use this search bar on top to locate everything related to your ads manager, your Facebook ads account and other information by entering a keyword or set of keywords.

Now, you can click on the menu tab icon located to the left to access the rest of the ad manager features. These include audience insights, a shortcut to the ads manager dashboard, your page posts, your analytics, your retargeting pixels, your saved assets such as saved audiences and images, as well as your billing.

Finally, you can click on the Facebook icon to the far left to go back to Facebook's home page, which is a helpful shortcut once you have finished setting up your campaigns. Tune in to my following chapter so i can show you how to create an awesome Facebook page from where you can run your ads!

Chapter 8: Creating A Facebook Page To Run Ads

Facebook pages are one of Facebook's best offerings for business. They are a versatile way for businesses to both maintain a presence on the platform from where to interact with people and as well as for advertising.

Because yeah, while it is true that adverts on Facebook can be run much like on any other advertising platform, in the form of display ads on the right hand menu, the best way to make the most out of Facebook's real estate is by advertising through pages.

So before showing you how to set up an ad campaign and how to set up actual Facebook ads, i want to show you how to properly create a Facebook page for your business, step by step. And you will have to start on Facebook's home page, click on the menu button, and then on the "create page" option from the menu.

Now, the first step when creating a Facebook page is to select the right page type. Page types include "local business or place" for brick and mortar businesses, "company, organization or institution" for corporate or organizational accounts, "brand or product" for specific brands, "artist, band or public figure" for performance artists, musicians, and the like, "entertainment" for specific pieces of entertainment media, and "cause or community" for non-profit causes.

Make sure to select an appropriate page type for your offers and business objective. In my case, i am going to select "brand or product" and then "website" from the "category" menu because i am going to promote offers and content from my "Diabetes Care Made Easy" website.

Enter your new page's name on the text field below this menu, and once you make your selection click on "get started" to continue. In the next step click on "upload a profile picture" to upload a profile picture for your page from your computer.

In the next step click on "upload a cover photo" to also add a nice looking and appropriate cover photo for your page. Now your page has been created, so it is time to start customizing it with your business and contact information.

Start by clicking on the three dotted button below the cover image and then click on the "edit page info" option. You can start by adding additional categories in the "categories" field to make it easier for people to find it when they use related keywords.

Now add a compelling, brief and to the point description in the "description" field. In both cases you will need to click on "save changes" after updating your information. Now scroll down to add your "contact" info, or click on the "contact" tab on top of the window.

Now, you have to specify how people can contact your business by checking the boxes corresponding to the contact method fields, which include "phone", "website", and "email". In this case, i am going to deselect the "has a phone number" option in the "phone" field because people can only contact us through my website and my email for the time being.

I then enter my website address in the "website" field and my main contact email address in the "email" field, and then i click on the "save changes" button corresponding to each instance.

You can also add an additional website address in the "additional links" field in case that your business is being promoted on another website, or in case that you have another website or landing page that you would like people visiting your page to click through.

Now scroll down to the "locations" part. Here you will be able to specify your exact location on a map by dragging and repositioning, and you can also enter your exact address on the "street address", "city" and "zip code" fields available above the map.

You can deselect the "has a street address" as well as the "customers visit my business at my street address" in case that your business is not location based. Make sure to save all your changes before closing this window.

Now your general page info and contact info have been updated, and you are ready to start receiving traffic from Facebook, which is an awesome, free way to get engagement as long as you keep your page alive with content.

Finally, you can add an extra layer of customization by adding a username to your page. Click on the "create a page username" link below the page's profile picture to get started. Now enter a username in the "username" field, make sure that it is available and then click on "create username".

Great! Now your page is all ready to properly go live! Tune in to my following chapter so i can show you how to create a compelling post that you can also promote right from your page's timeline!

Chapter 9: Promoting A Basic Page Post The Right Way

OK let's move onto the next step in your Facebook ads journey, creating an actual ad. The first type of ad that i am going to teach you to create is the simplest form of ad that you will be able to set up on Facebook.

And interestingly enough, you will not need to go to your ads manager in order to set one up because you will be able to create it and promote it right from your Facebook page. Yes, i am talking about promoted posts.

Promoted posts are page posts that you can boost by injecting them with some advertising dollars right after you create them. Granted, the majority of ads that i will teach you to set up in this training are page posts as well, but i will teach you how to create them using the advanced features on the ads manager.

But in this chapter i want to teach you the easiest way to promote a page post that you can use to increase the reach of a post by rapidly showing it to any target audience on its' members news feed right at the moment that you launch a post.

So to start creating a page post to promote start by going to your business page. You can reach your page by either clicking on the menu button on the top bar and then under "your pages", by checking the "your pages" menu on top of the right hand column, or by clicking on its corresponding icon in the "shortcuts" menu on the left.

Now, creating a page post for promotion should be approached the right way, as promoted posts should aim to get as much attention and positive engagement as possible, especially because you will be investing advertising money on them.

So let me show you how to create an engaging Facebook post that you can actually promote. First, you will have to go to the post space located on top of your page's timeline. Once there you will notice that the post is set as "status" by default, but promoted posts convert better when you add images to them.

You can click on "photo/video" to select how you want to insert media on your new post, and there are several options. In fact, the options available here are the same ones that you will be able to use when you create a news feed ad using the ads manager.

These options include "upload photo or video", "create photo album", "create slideshow", and create "canvas" if you wish to insert a combination of images and videos into your new promoted post.

Furthermore, if you insert a URL where you want to send people to in your page post, Facebook will fetch the images available on the landing page and insert them automatically into your post.

In my example case, i am going to insert my business website URL to promote the site and increase both brand awareness and clicks to my site through a simple page post. So i will start by inserting the URL in the "write something" field.

As you can see, Facebook just loaded the images from my site. What i have to do now is to select the image that i want to use to promote my site. My recommendation here for you is to select images with strong elements or backgrounds, and should not feature text.

To select your image you will need to deselect the ones that you are not going to feature, and you can do that by clicking on the "X" or "delete" icon on the upper right corner on each image or by clicking on the smaller thumbnails corresponding to each image below the post. Note that you can leave all images if you want to, but i do not recommend it, as the idea is to not saturate your post with information.

As you can see so far, this page post looks pretty awesome, with its feature image and website description which Facebook pulls right from your website. After inserting your URL and selecting your feature image, delete the URL text on the status field.

Now you will need to compose your post status, which is essentially your ad copy because this a promoted post. This description has to match your offer and the content in the landing page.

I am going to elaborate with my example post. Copy has to be brief and descriptive, so i am going to use the "Top-of-the-line Diabetes testing kits and proven treatment tips inside" copy line in the status.

Once you create your post, you have several options. On the drop down menu below the post you can select to "publish", "schedule", "backdate" or draft your post, so you will have to click on "publish".

Now that your new post is live you will see an option to "boost post". This option is what will allow you to promote your post right from your page, as soon as you publish it, so click on the "boost post" button to get started.

A "boost post" window will appear for you to set up your promoted post. One of the first things that you will notice is that there is a preview of how your promoted post will look on people's desktop and mobile feeds on the right side of this window.

On the left side is the actual set up. First you have to start by setting up your "objective". The "objective" is what you want to get as a result from promoting your post. In my case i am going to select "website visits" as my objective, but you might want to select "engagement" if you are more interested in getting reactions such as likes and comments.

Once you select your objective you will have to set up your "audience" below. You can start by clicking on the "edit" button from the "people you choose through targeting" option to edit your target audience.

You can also select an existing audience if you have previously saved one, or you can click on "create new audience" to set one up for this promoted post.

Scroll down once you set up your audience to set up your budget for this promoted post. Before specifying your total budget amount though i recommend you to select your ad duration first. There are three predefined durations: 1 day, 7 days, and 14 days. You can also select a custom duration by using the calendar function and selecting a specific date to stop showing your promoted post.

My recommendation here is to select a date that allows you to test your ad for 5 days. Now back to your total budget. My recommendation here is to set a total budget of $25 if you select a 5 day duration, so you can test out your promoted post on a $5 a day basis, and to increase your amount from there. If you select a different duration, enter a total budget that allows you to test your ad on a $5 a day basis.

Once you have all that set up click on "boost". You might be prompted to select your payment method if you haven't already. Once you do, click on "continue". Now your ad is ready to start running!

Chapter 10: Creating a basic ad using the ads manager

I hope that you are having a great time learning how to leverage the Facebook platform for your advertising efforts. So far i have been showing you how to locate the ad manager and how to create a basic page post to promote. In this chapter i am going to actually use the ad manager to create your first ad.

Start on your Facebook account, and from there click on the menu button on the top bar and then click on "create ads" and wait for your ads manager account to load.

Now that you are on your ads manager account it will take you a set of steps to create your first ad. You will land on the "campaign" selection screen by default every time that you open your ads manager as you can see here, which greatly simplifies the process.

You will be able "create a new campaign" or to "use existing campaign" if you already have one saved. In my example case i am are going to create a new campaign from scratch, as this is the first step of the ad creation process.

To create a new campaign you have to start by selecting your marketing objective. Your marketing objective is what you want to see as a result of creating a Facebook ads campaign, such as driving more sales on your online store, getting more traffic to your affiliate pages to increase affiliate offers, among others.

The objectives offered by Facebook ads include "brand awareness", "reach", "traffic", "engagement", "app installs", "video views", "lead generation", "messages", "conversions", "catalog sales", and store visits.

For my example case i am going to select one of the easiest to manage objectives available, one that is commonly used by most display ad network users. I am referring to the "reach" objective, which will allow me to show my ad to as many people as possible with my set budget.

OK, so once you have defined your objective, you will have to click on it. Then scroll down and name your new ad campaign in the "campaign name" field. Then click on the "set up add account" button.

On the next page you will have to specify your account country, your currency, and your time zone if you haven't done so already. Then click on "continue". Now you will be taken to the "ad set" section, where you will need to select the page you will be using to promote your ad, your audience, your ad placements, your budget and your schedule.

Here you will have to start by naming your new ad set in the "ad set name" field. In the "page" menu you will need to select the Facebook page that you will be using to promote your post. In this case, i am going to select the page that i just created recently.

Now you will have to scroll down to the "audience" column. Here you will have the option to either "create new audience" or "use a saved audience". For this chapter i am going to show you how to set up an audience from scratch, so i will select the "create new audience" option.

Start by selecting a location or series of locations in the "locations" section. Type the name of your target location in the text field above the map and click on it when it pops up. You can do so for as many locations you wish to target with your ad set.

You can further streamline your target location to your target audience by going to the "locations" menu and selecting whether to target "everyone in this location", "people who live in this location", "people recently in this location" or "people traveling to this location".

Now, in the "age" section you can select a base age and a top age to target. In the "gender" section you can select to either target "men", "women" or "all". And in the "languages" field you can type a specific language that you might want to target.

Of course, this all depends on what you are offering, so make sure to select the appropriate audience according to what you will be showing them in your ad.

Now, in the "detailed targeting" section you "include" or "exclude" people based on "demographics", "interests", and "behaviors". And in the "connections" section you can reach out to Facebook users according to the type of connection that they have with your page, such as "people who like your page" or "friends of people who like your page".

Finally, if you would like to target this same audience in a future campaign, you can click on the "save audience" button. Now to the "placements" column. In this column you can select "automatic placements" or "edit placements".

Selecting "Automatic placements" will serve your ads to all possible types of users on all types of devices across multiple networks which include third party networks. That is why i recommend you to select "edit placements" so you can select your own ad placements.

In this case, i am going to select "all devices" and i am going to deselect the "audience network" as well as the "messenger". Now in the "budget and schedule" column you have to set up both attributes for this new campaign. You can either select a "daily budget" if you want to spend a specific amount on a daily basis, or you can select "lifetime budget" if you want to spread a specific amount of money across several days.

In the "schedule" section you can select the "run my ad set continuously starting today" option to run your ad until you decide to stop it, or you can select the "set a start date and an end date" option to schedule how to run your new ad set.

Once again, my recommendation here is to set a "daily budget" of $5, or $10 if you can afford it, and then start increasing your daily amount until you find a sweet spot where you get good return on investment relative to your objective.

Now, i would prefer to select the "run my ad set continuously starting today" option in the "schedule" section to test out the ad set for five days, but you can schedule a 5 day period using the calendar functions as well.

Once you are done here click on "continue". In the following section you will have to edit your ad creative. Because everything else is already set up, you will need to start on the "format" section.

Here you will select the format of your ad. The "carousel" format allows you to insert 2 or more images and videos on your ad. The "single image" format will allow you to introduce a single image on your ad, just like the "single video" format will allow you to use a single video on your ad. Finally, you can select the "slideshow" format to create a looping video ad composed with up to 10 images.

For this chapter i am going to select the "single image" format. I am going to scroll down to the "images" section and click on the "browse library" to select an image for my ad. As you can see here, you will be able to select an image from your library, to select it from a collection of stock images or to "upload images" from your computer.

In this case i am going to select the image from my library that best reflects my offer. Once you make your selection click on "done". Let's now move to the "text" section. In this section you will insert your copy, your title and your URLs.

In the "text" field you have to enter your ad copy. Remember, your ad copy needs to be brief and to the point. In the "website URL" you will have to enter a URL if you will be promoting one, which is our case. You can uncheck the "add a website URL" option if you won't be promoting one.

Now, in the "headline" field you have to enter an attention

grabbing headline for your ad. In this case, i am going to enter the name of my business. And in the "news feed link description" i am going to type a very short but inciting call to action.

Now in the "call to action" menu you can actually select a working call to action button for your ad from the vast selection of calls to action available according to your offer. In this case, i am going to select the "no button" option.

You can always use the "ad preview" feature on the right to see how your ad is going to look on different placements, such as desktop and mobile feeds. Once you are done here click on the "confirm" button and wait for your ad to be approved.

And that's it! Join me in the following section so i can teach you some expert-level Facebook ad strategies!

Chapter 11: Creating A Custom Audience

Start on your Facebook account and load the ads manager through the "create ads" option in the options menu.

Once in the ads manager click on the menu icon on the top left corner of the dashboard. Now go to the "assets" column in the display menu and click on the "audiences" link. You will be taken to the "audiences" page, where you will be able to check, create and edit your target audiences.

To create a custom audience click on the "create audience" drop down menu above your saved audiences dashboard and then click on "custom audience". So what is a custom audience? A custom audience is an audience made of people that have a connection or relationship to your business.

Such an audience can be formed by people that have bought from you before, or people in your lists, or people that have engaged with your business before in one way or another, and that you can target with a Facebook ads campaign.

As you can see, there are several ways to target people with a custom audience. You can target people in a "customer file", which will allow you to target people according to customer or subscriber data saved on a file.

You can target "website traffic" by targeting lists of people that have visited your website, you can target people by "app activity", which is people who have used your app, you can target people by "offline activity", such as people that have bought from your offline store or that have provided you with a phone number for doing business, and you can target people by "engagement", which means people that have interacted with your content on Facebook.

The variety of custom targeting options is a welcome feature that will allow you to achieve faster results, and i am going to give you an example of how to set up a custom audience by creating a custom audience from a "customer file".

Once you choose to create a custom audience from a customer file you will be given the options to "add customers from your own file or copy and paste data", to "import from MailChimp" or to add a "customer file with lifetime value".

For my example i am going to use my own customer file, so i click on "add customers from my own file or copy and paste data". The first step is to "add customer list". To do this you can either "add a new file" or "copy and paste" the customer data.

In this case, i am going to upload a customer data file. If you decide to use a customer file, i recommend you to use the "download file template", to then open the file template and then to edit the data on the template according to your own data.

In this case, i am going to add a single test customer for this custom audience, and start by clearing all the placeholder data in the template that i am not going to edit over. Awesome. Now, i am only going to use my customer's email, first and last names, country of residence and gender as my customer data, so i clear all the attributes that i am not going to use as well.

I then edit the placeholder information and enter my own, and then save. Once saved, you can click on the "upload file" button to upload your saved file from your computer. Once uploaded click on "next".

Awesome. Now only make sure that the correct data is marked green, then click on "upload and create". Wait for your file to load and click on done. Great! Now your custom audience is saved. Apply these simple steps and never miss on an existing prospect!

Section 3

Chapter 12: Adding The Facebook Pixel From A Campaign To Your Business Website

I previously talked about how narrowing down your audience can help you to get better results, so i taught you how to create a custom audience. Now i am going to show you how to take that strategy a step further by teaching you how to add a Facebook Pixel to your business website.

What Is A Facebook Pixel?

A Facebook pixel is a tracking code that Facebook uses to track visitors of a website back to Facebook so it can show them targeted ads on their timelines. In other words, a Facebook pixel is a tracking code that works just like a tracking cookie, only that it works on the Facebook platform.

Have you noticed that when you go to certain business websites such as ecommerce sites and then go back to Facebook, you start seeing ads promoting those websites on your timeline? That is the Facebook pixel at work. What the pixel did was track you from the websites that you visited back to Facebook, where the businesses that manage those websites bid for ad space on your timeline.

How To Add The Facebook Pixel To Your Own Site

Adding the Facebook pixel to your own website is quite easy, and i am going to show you how, step by step. First you have to start by logging in to your Facebook account, and from there go to the ads manager by clicking on the top bar menu and then on "create ads".

Now go and click on the tools menu, then click on the "pixels" link under the "measure and report" section. You will be taken to the "Facebook Pixels" page. Once there click on the "create a pixel" button. A pop up window will appear with your account's pixel information, and you will need to click on the "create" button.

Awesome! Now that you have created your Facebook Pixel, you can start using it on your website. And in order to use your pixel on your website, you have to install it there. As you can see, there are three ways to install your Facebook pixel on your page.

You can "use an integration or tag manager" such as the "Google tag manager" and other third party integration platforms. You can "manually insert the code yourself" by copying the pixel code and inserting it on your website, and you can "mail instructions to a developer" that can take care of the pixel for you.

Just as promised, i am going to show you how to add your new pixel to your business website the easy way. Start by clicking on the "manually install the code yourself" option. Now scroll down until you find your Facebook Pixel code, which looks like this, and then click on it to copy it to your clipboard.

Once you copy your Facebook pixel code go to your website's main dashboard. Now what you have to do is to paste your pixel code in the header section of your website. To do that you have to access your site's header code.

For this example i am going to use my own WordPress website. There are two ways to add this pixel code to a WordPress site. The easiest method is by using the "insert headers and footers" plugin.

To use this plugin to add your pixel to your site you will have to hover over the "plugins" tab on your WordPress dashboard, and then to click on the "add new" option. Now type "insert headers and footers" in the "search plugins" search bar.

Locate the plugin in the search results and click on the "install now" button, then click on "activate" once it installs. Now hover over the "settings" tab on the dashboard left-hand menu and click on the "insert headers and footers" option.

Now paste your pixel code in the "scripts in header" field and click on "save". The second method is by actually adding it to the header section of your site's code yourself. Hover over the "appearance" tab on the left-hand menu and click on the "editor" option. Now go to the "templates" menu on the right, locate "theme header" and click on it.

Now paste your code between the "<head>" and "</head>" tags like i just did and click on "update file". Once you have added your code by using either method go back to where you left on Facebook and enter your website's URL in the "send test traffic to your pixel" field and click on the "send test traffic" button.

Awesome! Your Facebook pixel is now active on your site, so click on "continue". In the following step you will have to "add your events". This means that you have to specify what types of actions do you want your Facebook pixel to track on your site.

The Facebook pixel will allow you to track actions such as purchases, generated leads, registrations, payment info added by customers, items added to a shopping cart or wish list, initiated checkouts, searches and content views.

Once you have selected which actions to track on your site click on "done". And that is it! You will start seeing activity from your pixel once it starts retargeting people with Facebook ads, so keep an eye on it!

Chapter 13: Sending More Traffic To Your Site With Facebook Ad

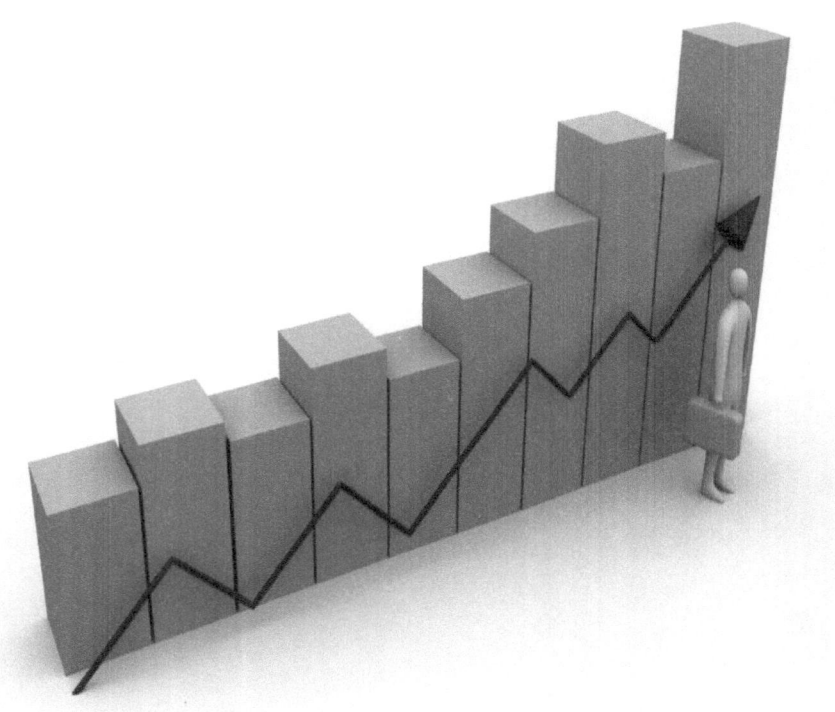

Sending traffic to your website is a top marketing objective regardless of what your end objective is. Whether you want to drive more sales, or to get more registrations, or to generate more leads, you will not be able to successfully achieve those objectives if you don't first generate traffic.

And generating traffic is not easy. More importantly, generating qualified traffic is harder still. But the good news is that i am here to help you out with that, and in this chapter i am going to teach you how to send more traffic to your site with Facebook ads.

Start by going to your ads manager account. Once in your ads manager dashboard select "traffic" as your marketing objective. Now name your new ad campaign. Now click on the "ad set" tab on the left-hand menu.

Here you will be editing your ad set. Start by giving a name to your new ad set in the "ad set name". Now select your "traffic" destination. This is where you want to send traffic to with your Facebook ads. You can send traffic to a "website", to an "app, or to your business's Facebook page messenger. You will be using this ad to send traffic to your site, so select "website" to continue.

Now, when you select "traffic" as your marketing objective, you will have the option to set up offers to drive traffic to your target destination by turning on the "offer" option. You will need to select from which page you will be promoting an offer to and click on "create offer".

You then will be able to enter your "offer title", your "offer details", an "end date" and "end time" for your offer. You will also be able to select whether to let your customers to redeem your offer "online", "in store" or "both".

Then you will be able generate redemption codes for your offer, to specify how many codes you will give away, and to enter your offer terms and conditions. Once you finalize your offer you have to click on "create". For this example i am going to focus on the ad set up.

Now you have to set up your "audience". Now, in order to get as much traffic as possible, you have to select the regions where people are more likely to respond to your offer, taking into account demographic factors such as language, genders, ages and interests.

In this case, i want to send more traffic to my "Diabetes Care Made Easy" website, so i need to start by selecting locations such as the United States, the United Kingdom and Australia. Now i am going to click on the "locations" menu and select "people who live in this location".

This is an important detail to target because i want to show my ads to people most likely to respond to the ad, and people traveling or visiting the location can be considered mobile individuals, and they're unlikely to respond to my ads, especially if they don't talk the language in the target regions.

I now select an age range between "29" and "65" to target users that are likely to be interested in my content. I then select "all" genders and select "English" as my target language. Please note that these settings will immensely depend on what your content, your offers and your target demographics, so they will vary for you.

Now, in the "detailed targeting" section you can "include" or "exclude" people by demographics, interests, behaviors and other categories. In my example case, i am going to include people that are interested in "healthy food", and i will exclude people that are interested in "junk food".

In the "connections" menu you can select to target people by how they are connected to your pages, your apps and your events. I am not going to use these "connections" in my audience, so i now move to the "placements" section.

You can either select "automatic placements" to show your ads in every placement possible or to "edit placements" to select your ad placements yourself. My recommendation here is to edit your placements and to deselect the "audience network" and the "messenger" options to avoid getting to many fake clicks from bots.

Now scroll down and set up your "budget and schedule". My recommendation here is to set up a "daily budget" of $5 and to "set a start and an end date" of five days so you can test how your ads perform, and then to go up from there.

Once you set up your budget and schedule click on "continue". Now it is time to create your ad. Start by giving a name to your ad in the "ad name" field. Then select whether to "create new ad" or "use existing post".

In this example case i am going to guide you through creating a new ad. Start by selecting the Facebook page that you are going to use to send your ads. Now select your ad format.

You can use the "carousel" format to insert 2 or more images and videos in your ad, the "single image" format to introduce a single image on your ad, the "single video" format to insert a single video on your ad. Finally, you can use the "slideshow" format to create a looping video ad with up to 10 images.

For this example case i am going to select the "single image" format. So click on "browse library" to select an image for your ad. Now select your ad image and click on "done". Now scroll down and enter your website's URL in the "website URL" field.

Now enter a brief headline text in the "headline" field. In this case i am going to use the "Diabetes care, just made easier" text as my headline.

Now, in the "text" field you have to enter a brief copy that is enticing enough as to encourage clicks, and it will be enough to compose text copy with intriguing text, a question, or an offer such as a discount or coupon. That is why in my case i am are going to use the "Want to know what is affecting your health as well as your wallet?" text.

In the "call to action" menu you have to select a call to

action button for your ad. In this case, i am going to select the "learn more" call to action.

I recommend you to enter a brief description about the content of your offer or website in the "newsfeed link description" field, as Facebook pulls text from your site that might look out of place on your ad.

Now preview your ad, make sure that everything is OK and click on "confirm". Then wait for your ad to be approved. And that's it! i will be showing you how to increase conversions on your website with Facebook ads next, so tune in!

Chapter 14: Increasing Conversions Through The Ads Manager

Let's keep on setting up the customer journey with Facebook ads. Now that you know how to set up ads to send traffic to your website it is time for you to learn how to drive actual conversions from all the traffic that you will get!

Start on your ads manager dashboard and select "conversions" as your marketing objective. To name your new ad campaign and click on the "ad set" tab on the left-hand menu.

Now name your new ad set in the "ad set name" field and move to the "conversion" section. First select "website" as your conversion destination. Now click on the "please select a conversion event" field to select a conversion objective from the conversion list menu. In this case i am going to select "view content" as our target conversion.

You can activate "offers" on your ads when you select "conversions" as your marketing objective. In this case i am not going to activate "offers" in our ad, so i continue to the "audience" section.

Start by selecting your locations, then click on the "locations" menu and select "people who live in this location". Now select an age range, then select "genders" and enter your target language.

Please remember that you can "include" or "exclude" people by demographics, interests, behaviors and other categories in the "detailed targeting" section.

I am going to use the same information that i used in my previous campaign, so i am going to "include" people that are interested in "healthy food", and i will "exclude" people that are interested in "junk food".

I recommend you to save an audience set-up in case you plan to use the same audience information in future campaigns. To do so click on the "save this audience" button, name your campaign and click on "save".

Now go to the "placements" section. Once again, my recommendation here is to edit your placements and to deselect the "audience network" and the "messenger" options to avoid non-converting clicks.

Now go to the "budget and schedule" section. Again, my recommendation here is to set up a "daily budget" of $5 and to "set a start and an end date" of five days to test out your campaign. Then click on "continue".

Now it is time to create your ad. Start by giving a name to your ad in the "ad name" field. Then select whether to "create new ad" or "use existing post". In this case, i am going to "use an existing post" that can work well with my "view content" conversion strategy.

When you select to "use existing post" you will have to select the Facebook page that you are going to use to serve your ads, then you will have to "select a page post" on the "creative" section.

You can then preview your ad to make sure that everything is OK and click on "confirm". Then wait for your ad to be approved. And that's it!

Chapter 15: Creating A Facebook Retargeting Campaign

I talked in depth about what is retargeting and how it works on Facebook, and now it is time to tell you how to actually set-up a retargeting campaign yourself. Start by going to your ads manager.

Once there click on the menu button on the top left corner and then click on the "audiences" link in the "assets" section of the menu. Now click on the "create audience" and select "custom audience".

Now select "website traffic" on the "create a custom audience" window. The reason why you are going to select this option is because retargeting works by tracking the people that visit your website back to Facebook, where you are going to directly retarget them with your ads.

Please note that in order to set up a retargeting campaign you will need to install your Facebook pixel on your website first, which is what will allow you to retarget your visitors on Facebook. Thankfully, i already have that covered, so let's continue.

Now you have to select how to retarget your site's visitors according to specific criteria. You can retarget "all website visitors" and select how many days after they have visited your site you will retarget them.

You can select "people who have visited specific web pages" on your site and enter a specific URL from your site from where to track your visitors. This will allow you to qualify interested visitors according to content specific to those pages.

You can select "visitors by time spent" to retarget visitors that have spent a certain percentage of time on your site. Lastly, you can select retargeting criteria from your pixel events on the "from your events" sub menu.

You can click on "further narrow" to add more retargeting criteria, or on "exclude" to add criteria that excludes visitors from being retargeted if they take action on your excluding criteria.

If you select two or more retargeting criteria you can then "include people who meet" "any" of the criteria to track visitors who have taken action on any of your selected criteria or "include people who meet" "all" criteria to only track visitors who have taken action on each of your selected criteria.

After you have selected your criteria you can then name your custom retargeting audience in the "audience name" field and then click on "create audience", then click on "done".

Awesome! Now that your custom retargeting audience is set up you can use it on your ad campaigns. You will have to select your objective and then name your new retargeting campaign.

Once on the "ad set" section you will have to click on the "custom audiences" field while setting up your "audience" and select your custom retargeting audience.

Then you will have to proceed with the ad creation process. The results will be that your new Facebook ad will be served to people who have visited your website according to your retargeting criteria. And that is it! Now you will be able to reach your website visitors on Facebook too!

Chapter 16: Creating A Lead-Generation Funnel

Once you start running Facebook ads for a while you realize that, as awesome as they are, your Facebook ads are not enough for generating new leads, and that you need to optimize your plan. The good news is that i am here to you help you out, so listen up!

Step One – Attract Visitors

This step is a no-brainer, really, as i already showed you how to attract lots of visitors to your website the easy way, but here are some additional tips.

For one, focus your message on your audience's needs and interests, on their problems and the solutions that you offer to their problems through your products or services. Then narrow your creative message down to what people in your audience will gain by visiting your website. Or you can also tell your audience about the problems that they will face if they don't visit your website to find a solution.

Both are powerful click-drivers! Then target a broad audience with your ads.

Step Two – Generate Leads

Once you take people to your site through your ads you have to capture them, and the best strategy will always be to use a lead magnet. Now, your ad copy will do half the job of telling your potential leads about the lead magnet on your site.

So you will need to add a clear "call to action" button on your ad by selecting an appropriate call to action on the "call to action" menu while setting up your ad. For example, if your lead magnet is an eBook, you should use the "download" call to action button on your ad.

Yet the focus on this step should be on your lead magnet. eBooks, webinars, giveaways, and reports are all great lead magnets!

Step 3- Convert

Now that your most interested visitors have converted into leads you can create a retargeting campaign to retarget visitors who have signed up to claim your lead magnet and create an ad with an offer for them.

Now, to drive conversions such as sales through an ad you should promote an offer that is hard to put down, such as a heavily discounted package.

Step 4 – Adopt Promoters

To keep generating leads you can create retargeting campaigns to reach the people that have spent money on your business to offer them a reward. Marketing studies have found that customers that receive rewards become loyal to the point of promoting the brand rewarding them. This will allow you to generate leads from people who have already converted to your business. Apply these strategies and you won't ever run out of leads again!

Section 4

Chapter 17: Do's and Don'ts

Do's

Do Define Your Goal First

One way to avoid being overwhelmed by the Facebook Ads platform is by defining your objective upfront. Once you map out your strategy and define your goal it will be easier for you to select an objective when you start setting up your campaigns.

Do Personalize Your Campaigns

Select audiences that make sense to your offer and your objective and give them the right type of incentive. This will give you a greater chance of increasing conversions.

Do Your Research

One of the best ways to make sure that you are successful on each new campaign that you launch is by researching the results of similar brands promoting similar products on Facebook ads.

Do Take Care of Copy

Advertising copy has to be brief and persuading. Don't go beating around the bush and describe your offer to the point. That encourages people to take action on the spot!

Do Follow Up

Once you convert customers with your Facebook ads make sure to follow them up with incentives such as prizes and discounts to build an engaging relationship.

Do Split Test Your Campaigns

Always test two or more variations of the same campaign, each one with different targets, or different copy, or different design elements, or both.

Do Use High Quality Assets

It is not only important to use images, videos and icons on your ads to make them pop up on the timeline, it is also important that they are of the highest quality possible.

Do Always Include A Call To Action

It's always safe to include a call to action that leads to your objective to increase click throughs, even when you think that an ad does not call for one.

Do Monitor Your Active Campaigns

The best way to learn about how to properly optimize your campaigns is to monitor them while they are running, so make sure to track them daily through your ads manager.

Do Retarget

Facebook is the only platform that allows you to serve and retarget from the same service, so don't forget to add your pixel to your site to retarget visitors.

Don'ts

Don't Use White Backgrounds on Ads

The background color on the Facebook feed is white, so using white or light backgrounds is the easiest way to encourage users to scroll past your ads!

Don't Use Vague Stock Images

If you use stock images for your ads, always make sure that they are relevant to your offer and your copy, otherwise the potential customer will be confused at what your ad is all about.

Don't Overuse Sales Posts

Do not use Facebook ads to sell your products. Instead, use them to tell a story about the benefits of your products and add a call to action that takes users to your sales page without telling them to "buy now".

 ### Don't Use Facebook Ads for B2B advertising

Facebook ads are not that effective when it comes to advertising to other businesses because almost all businesses are using Facebook to find and nurture customers.

 ### Don't Clutter The Newsfeed

Posting too many ads to the same users everyday several times a day is the easiest way to get your promoted posts blocked. Doing so will also deplete your budget pretty fast, so don't!

Don't Use The Audience Network

One of the placements available for you to serve your ads is the audience network, but we advise against you using this option because, on one hand, you won't be able to track your results accurately on this placement, and secondly, most of the clicks you'll get from it are from bots!

 ### Don't Neglect Your Facebook Page

It is not enough to only create posts to promote, so make sure to post relevant content on a regular basis to keep your business page alive and your customers engaged.

 ### Don't Target Too Broadly

Be specific about your target audience and its attributes, as your ads will be deemed irrelevant by people in the wrong audience.

 ### Don't Over Use Text

Text in your Facebook ads should be limited to your copy, and if you have to include text in your ad image make sure that it only reflects a keyword or number. Save phrases and other stuff for the landing page!

Chapter 18: Premium tools and Services to consider

Wordstream

"Wordstream" is an online based social management software that will allow you to revamp your Facebook advertising workflow through prescriptive alerts that are customized for the Facebook ads platform, among many other performance-boosting features.

Hootsuite

"Hootsuite" is an all-in-one social media scheduling platform with awesome features for Facebook advertisers, such as automating the ad creation workflow by evaluating the content on the user's Facebook pages and then creating ads based on that same content!

Qwaya

"Qwaya" is another all-in-one tool that can greatly simplify your workflow. It has a built-in ad scheduler, manual ad rotation functionalities, URL builder, split testing functionalities, multiple ad templates, a campaign organizer, and full integration with third party platforms such as Google Analytics!

Pagemodo

"Pagemodo" is a great advertising tool that provides Facebook advertisers with a wide selection of ad templates, free of royalty images and a powerful ad builder. It also has built-in targeting, segmentation, analytics and performance tools!

KISSmetrics

"KISSmetrics" is behavioral-analytics tool for advertisers. The power of KISSmetrics is in providing you with crucial data about the performance of your Facebook advertising campaigns by contextualizing such data with broader data points to give you the most accurate insights possible!

AdEspresso

"AdEspresso" is a simplified analytics platform specially designed for Facebook advertisers. In fact, it is considered to be one of the simplest, more straightforward analytics tools for digital marketers, and it offers easy to understand visual analytics, customizable dashboards, and very detailed metrics.

Social Ads Tool

"Social Ads Tool" is a great platform for advertising partners that service business owners because it truly delivers lead generation success. It offers automatic ad customizations, deep reporting, conversion tracking and timeline updates.

Driftrock

"Driftrock" is one of the highest regarded social advertising tools. Some of its more awesome features include signal-triggered ads, optimization automation, and lead response.

AdRoll

"AdRoll" is a Facebook remarketing tool that provides you access to high-level retargeting features such as cross-device targeting, helping you to better channel your Facebook retargeting efforts.

AdSpringr

"AdSpringr" is an advanced ad creation tool for e-businesses that also offers analysis and performance reporting, optimization, high-level targeting, automated client reporting, automated graphical reporting and visual representation of important Facebook marketing parameters.

Chapter 19: Shocking Case Studies

Noah Kagan: "Noah Kagan" is an American entrepreneur focusing his efforts on internet marketing. He is the founder of "Appsumo" and "SumoMe".

Objective: His objective was to simply drive people to his opt-ins to later engage them and encourage them to try his products.

Strategy: He used Facebook ads to increase traffic to his website, promote his opt-in on his landing page and then promote his products to subscribers.

Results: He got net profits of $267 from selling his course after investing $3 on each email lead!

Design Pickle: "Design Pickle" is a graphic design company that provides unlimited designs for a monthly fee.

Objective: Their objective was to promote their unusual service following the "no credit card required" free trial method.

Strategy: They directed their Facebook ads traffic to a long-form sign up form to properly capture the leads most likely to be interested in the service. They also integrated the Facebook pixel on their sign up page to retarget visitors that didn't complete the sign up.

Results: 17 out of 30 new clients were generated by retargeting!

[Buffer](): "Buffer" is a popular social media management platform.

Objective: Their objective was to see what kind of results they could achieve by investing only $5 a day on Facebook ads as to have a better outlook on how small businesses can make the most out of small budgets.

Strategy: They tested their $5 ad spend on different objectives such as page likes, clicks to website and boosted posts.

Results: They netted 9 likes per day, 1 click through per day and 787 new people reached with boosted posts per each $5 spent on each objective!

Tough Mudder: "Tough Mudder" is an obstacle course challenge that originated in Brooklyn, New York, and that is now rocking all over the world.

Objective: The community-driven initiative's objective was to reach new participants and engage them through social media.

Strategy: The used Facebook ads to target a highly targeted audience to engage them with video footage taken directly from the races.

Results: 20% of "Tough Mudder" participants were influenced to sign up for the obstacle course challenge through Facebook ads!

Fitbit: "Fitbit" is a lifestyle brand focused on creating health and fitness oriented products that can change people's lives.

Objective: The company's objective was to increase their level of engagement as well as traffic to their site.

Strategy: They used Facebook ads to boost posts that redirected people to articles on the Fitbit blog.

Results: "Fitbit" got 75,000 engagements on Facebook during a single month in 2015 after using this strategy!

Brian Carter: "Brian Carter" is a prominent marketer and advertising expert that specializes in social media.

Objective: Carter wanted to know what kind of beneficial results he could get if he started a Facebook advertising campaign on the smallest budget possible.

Strategy: He invested $1 a day on impressions during a 30 day period.

Results: Carter was able to reach a total of 120,000 people on a $30 monthly budget, which means that he reached 4,000 a day for $1, which demonstrates that Facebook is the cheapest advertising alternative.

SamCart: "SamCart" is an ecommerce software company founded by Brian Moran.

Objective: Brian's objective was to generate as many leads as possible with Facebook ads.

Strategy: He used Facebook ads to sell his courses and raining products, and he targeted his existing email lists, a lookalike version of his email list, and a custom audience.

Results: he invested a total of $8,240 and got $14,081 of sales in return!

[Veeroll](): "Veeroll" is a video advertising platform that allows its users to generate video ads the easy way.

Objective: Veeroll's objective was to break the mold and use Facebook ads to generate leads for "Business to Business" or "B2B" companies.

Strategy: They used video ads to send traffic to a webinar funnel.

Results: The company was able to generate 122 sign ups that resulted in $11,000 of monthly revenue in only two weeks!

Paul Ramondo: "Paul Ramondo" is a digital marketer that specializes in Facebook Ads and in creating digital advertising funnels that work for any niche.

Objective: His objective was to devise a Facebook Ad sales funnel that starts by building a connection with the client before going for the sale.

Strategy: He started by showing his ads to his existing audience to allow Facebook to first give his ads a high relevancy score. He then promoted a lead magnet with content related to one of his client's products. Lastly, he showed a sales ad to those that opted in through the ads.

Results: Paul invested $5,989 in ad spend, and got a staggering $163,969 of sales in return!

Persuasion Nation: "Persuasion Nation" is a digital marketing blog run by Mary Fernandez, a blogging strategist and persuasion psychology fanatic.

Objective: Mary wanted to generate as many blog subscribers for her clients as possible, on the cheap.

Strategy: Mary started personalizing her clients' ads. For example, she would feature a photo or video of her clients in the ads.

Results: Using personalized assets in the ads proved to be a top strategy, as people responded way better to them, which led Mary to discover that she could easily get new blog subscribers for any niche for only $0.43 by using video ads!

Chapter 20: Frequently Asked Questions

What Is "Facebook User Value"?

It is the cost of reaching a user through advertising. For instance, users that use Facebook for hours a day, that like and follow lots of pages, and that click on lots of ads are more expensive on average.

What Type Of Results Should You Expect From Using Facebook Ads?

Your end results will largely depend on your chosen objective and your overall performance. Other factors such as your budget and niche will also play a role. I recommend you to select the objective that best matches what you want to achieve through your Facebook ads to get a direct reading of your results.

Where Should You Position Your Ads?

There are only two possible placements for ads on Facebook: either on the right hand column or on the news feed. Ads on the right hand column tend to get more clicks because people know they're adverts, but they're less likely to convert than ads on the news feed, although that depends on what you are promoting. Right hand ads work better for direct sales ads, and news feed ads work better for promoting content.

How Much Should You Spend on Facebook Ads?

There are marketers out there who get awesome results because they're spending thousands of dollars on their campaigns, and if your budget allows for it, you can and totally should go that route. However, you can start on a $5-30 daily budget and go up from there, as that is the sweet spot for trying out your new ad campaigns on the platform.

What Kind of Bidding Strategy Should You Select?

Your bidding strategy should be directly tied to your objective. Do you want to make more sales? Bid for conversions. Do you want to increase website traffic? Bid for Cost-Per-Clicks. Do you want to show your ads to as many people as possible to test the waters? Bid for Cost-Per-Mile.

What Is The Relevance Score?

The relevance score is a metric that will allow you to know how relevant your ad is to your target audience. It goes from 1 to 10, and it is not determined by how good looking your ad is, but by how relevant it is to the people that you are serving it to.

An ideal relevance score shouldn't be less than 8. If your ads have a relevance score that is lower than 8, it means that you should either optimize your ad for your target audience, or to modify the audience that you are targeting.

What Type of Mistakes Can Lose You Conversions?

The most common cause of lost conversions is in landing page mistakes. And the most common include landing page designs that leave a bad first impression, calls to action and ads that send different messages, broad targeting, poor mobile optimization, and no images on the landing page.

How Fast Do Facebook Ads Work?

The average time at which a person responds and decides to convert after seeing an advert is 90 seconds, so take that into consideration when creating your ads.

Are There Any Factors Affecting Your Metrics That You Should Be Aware of?

"Junk" Clicks from mobile devices is a factor affecting your metrics because click throughs from mobile devices too often include taps made by mistake such as when a user is using a device with a small screen. Also, clicks from duplicates accounts or dummy accounts can affect an accurate reading of your metrics.

How Can You Avoid "Junk" Clicks?

The only solution is perhaps by skipping mobile advertising, which isn't that bad in most cases, especially if you are promoting squeeze pages or want more website traffic.

Conclusion:

I am thrilled that you have chosen to take advantage of my Training Guide, and i wish you amazing success.

And in order to take your Facebook Ads Efforts even farther, i invite you to get the most out of it by getting access to the top resources attached here.

Thanks so much for the time you have dedicated to learning how to get the most advantages from Facebook Advertising.

Facebook Ads have come to stay in the market forever.

To Your Success,

Top Resources

Videos
https://www.youtube.com/watch?v=PMC-R28Ev6E
https://www.youtube.com/watch?v=HI-Az637jsI

Tools & Services
https://www.facebook.com/business/news/upgraded-ad-tools
http://www.socialadstool.com/

Training Courses
https://www.udemy.com/facebook-ads-course-beginner-to-advanced/
www.youtube.com/embed/zmqtGXN20bE

Blogs
https://blog.tryadhawk.com/facebook-ads/4-of-the-best-facebook-ad-tools/
https://adespresso.com/blog/

Forums
https://www.warriorforum.com/tags/facebook%20ads.html
https://www.blackhatworld.com/tags/facebook-ads/

Affiliate Programs
https://www.jvzoo.com/
http://www.jvshare.com/

Webinars
https://adespresso.com/webinars/
http://www.cpcstrategy.com/2017-q4-facebook-advertising-summit-webinar-recording/

Infographics
https://www.invespcro.com/blog/facebook-advertising-statistics/
http://www.pagemodo.com/blog/your-2017-small-business-guide-to-facebook-ads-infographic/

Case Studies
https://aggregateblog.com/best-facebook-ad-examples/
https://www.facebook.com/business/success/categories/financial-services

Facts
http://www.jeffbullas.com/23-extraordinary-facebook-advertising-facts/
http://www.soravjain.com/facebook-linkedin-stats-facts-2017

www.ingramcontent.com/pod-product-compliance
Lightning Source LLC
Chambersburg PA
CBHW031436210526
45464CB00005B/2229